A Note to Parents & Teachers—

Welcome to I See Insects from Xist Publishing! These books are designed to inspire discovery and delight in the youngest readers. Each book features very simple sentences with visual cues to help beginners read their very first text.

You can help each child develop a lifetime love of reading right from the very start. Here are some ways to help a beginning reader get going:

 Read the book aloud as a first introduction

 Run your fingers below the words as you read each line

 Give the child the chance to finish the sentences or read repeating words while you read the rest.

 Encourage the child to read aloud every day!

Copyright © Xist Publishing 2022
First Edition
All Rights Reserved.
No portion of this book may be reproduced without express permission from the publisher.

Published proudly in the State of Texas, USA by Xist Publishing
www.xistpublishing.com
24200 Southwest Freeway Suite 402- 290 Rosenberg, TX 77471
All images licensed from Adobe Stock
First Edition

Perfect Bound ISBN: 978-1-5324-4143-1
Saddle Stitch ISBN: 978-1-5324-2857-9
Hardcover ISBN: 978-1-5324-3340-5
eISBN: 978-1-5324-2832-6

I See Insects
Cricket

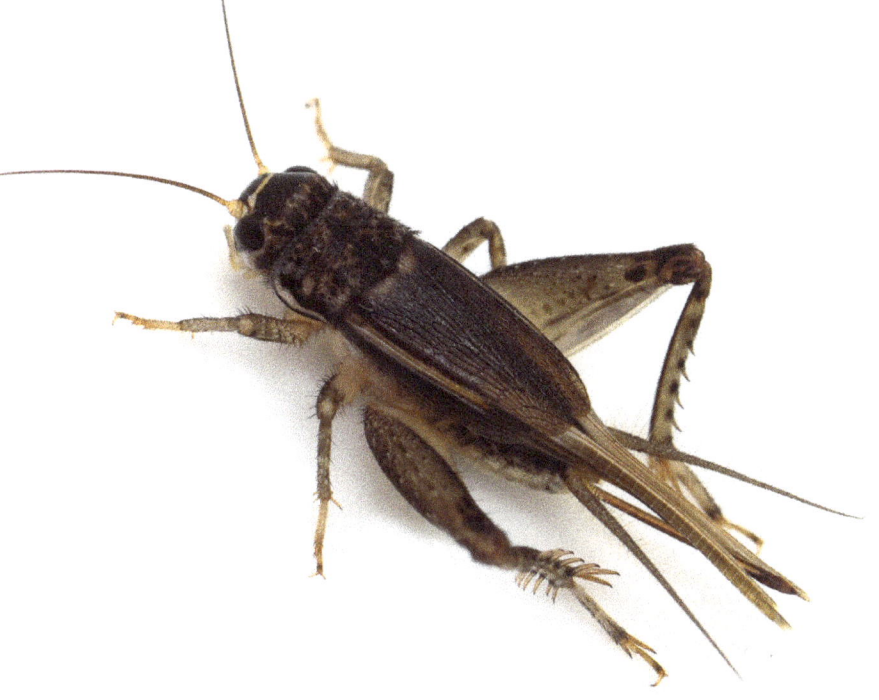

written by **August Hoeft**

xist Publishing
INSPIRING DISCOVERY & DELIGHT

I see a cricket.

The cricket is brown.

The cricket has six legs.

The cricket eats fruit.

The cricket lives on plants.

I see a cricket.

Things to do next!

Write a Sentence

I see a _____.

Drawing

Make a drawing of your favorite insect.

Sharing

Talk to your classmates about your favorite picture in this book. Explain to them why you like it.

WORD LIST

a	legs
brown	lives
cricket	on
eats	plants
fruit	see
has	six
I	the
is	